FREEDOM
FROM
ADDICTION

Story of Redemption and Forgiveness

GREGORY BEDNER LLPC, MA

WESTBOW®
PRESS
A DIVISION OF THOMAS NELSON
& ZONDERVAN

Scripture taken from the New King James Version. Copyright 1979, 1980, 1982 by Thomas Nelson, inc. Used by permission. All rights reserved.

Scriptures taken from the Holy Bible, New International Version®, NIV®. Copyright © 1973, 1978, 1984, 2011 by Biblica, Inc.™ Used by permission of Zondervan. All rights reserved worldwide. www.zondervan.com The "NIV" and "New International Version" are trademarks registered in the United States Patent and Trademark Office by Biblica, Inc.™ All rights reserved.

Scripture quotations are from The Holy Bible, English Standard Version® (ESV®), copyright © 2001 by Crossway, a publishing ministry of Good News Publishers. Used by permission. All rights reserved.

Scripture quotations taken from the Holy Bible, New Living Translation, Copyright © 1996, 2004. Used by permission of Tyndale House Publishers, Inc., Wheaton, Illinois 60189. All rights reserved.

WestBow Press books may be ordered through booksellers or by contacting:

WestBow Press
A Division of Thomas Nelson & Zondervan
1663 Liberty Drive
Bloomington, IN 47403
www.westbowpress.com
1 (866) 928-1240

Because of the dynamic nature of the Internet, any web addresses or links contained in this book may have changed since publication and may no longer be valid. The views expressed in this work are solely those of the author and do not necessarily reflect the views of the publisher, and the publisher hereby disclaims any responsibility for them.

Any people depicted in stock imagery provided by Thinkstock are models, and such images are being used for illustrative purposes only. Certain stock imagery © Thinkstock.

ISBN: 978-1-4908-4106-9 (sc)
ISBN: 978-1-4908-4107-6 (hc)
ISBN: 978-1-4908-4105-2 (e)

Library of Congress Control Number: 2014910618

Printed in the United States of America.

WestBow Press rev. date: 07/01/2014

Preface

I wanted to write a book that could help bring freedom to those struggling with addiction. Addiction is a spiritual disease that causes devastation to the user and those who come in contact with the addict. Many young men and women are walking blindly to their graves. We all have a purpose in life, and addiction is the destroyer of dreams. Addiction takes the lives of many of our youth each year. It destroys more homes than anything else. Addiction leads to a life of misery, and it brings suffering to those involved. Family members watch as their children lose their battles with addiction every day. It has touched my life in more ways than one.

I want to tell my story.

My story is that of a son who walked away from his father and returned home a victor. I decided I was going to keep this book simple. It would take a lifetime for me to present all I have learned about myself in my spiritual journey toward freedom. This book is not the end but the beginning—the beginning of self-discovery.

The road to recovery is long and full of hills and valleys. Growing toward the likeness of my Creator and being set free from addiction has been a joyous journey. In this book, I touch on fear and the negative consequences of not being able to deal with it effectively. I focus on building self-worth, because those who don't feel good about themselves have no reason to fight. I focus on anger and resentment, because these two areas have caused many people to fail and relapse. I focus on building a good support system because surrounding myself with others that are on the same path and being around others who will hold me accountable is important. When you hang out in Rome you will do as the Romans. We surround ourselves with those who will put us in the best position to succeed. Believe me you don't want to be around people who are not on the same mission. Changing old friends and old hang outs is difficult for most addicts. Change is difficult. There are times that I am around drinking. During Christmas parties my family is known to drink. The point is that all my relatives know I have a problem and when I get uncomfortable I leave. I take an honest look at my reasons for being in any situation. I focus on selfishness and how a selfless life brings freedom. I focus on forgiveness, because nothing brings us closer to peace and serenity than letting go of resentments. I discuss peace, because without peace this book would have never been written.

Figuring out the key areas I wanted to focus on was the hardest part of writing this book. Sobriety is about change and growing. It is about finding freedom and peace. It is about self-searching and trying to embrace a different life. I have learned so much about myself since I started this journey toward change and freedom. I have learned to feel good about myself, and I have learned to love others. Drugs supplied me with a false sense of security, and in the end I found true strength in God through a relationship with Jesus Christ. The goal of this book is to show how I recovered from drug addiction and found peace, strength, and purpose.

I ultimately focus on the author of this book: Jesus Christ. I believe the Lord wanted me to write this book. I believe in a loving God who is tired of seeing his children suffer and die. I have found freedom and true peace in the loving arms of my Creator.

I wrote this book from my perspective in the hopes that others could relate to me and find the same power I did. I give my opinion on why someone would want to quit using drugs and alcohol. I believe this book will change lives. I work as a substance abuse counselor and feel as though it is my mission in life to help those who are suffering to find their way out.

God wants his children to be free and live life more abundantly. What is your purpose here on earth? Freedom from addiction is attainable. Living a life of peace and purpose is wonderful.

CHAPTER 1
My Story

The Parable of the Lost Son

Jesus continued: There was a man who had two sons. The younger one said to his father, "Father, give me my share of the estate." So he divided his property between them.

Not long after that, the younger son got together all he had, set off for a distant country and there squandered his wealth in wild living. After he had spent everything, there was a severe famine in that whole country, and he began to be in need. So he went and hired himself out to a citizen of that country, who sent him to his fields to feed pigs. He longed to fill his stomach with the pods that the pigs were eating, but no one gave him anything.

When he came to his senses, he said, "How many of my father's hired servants have food to spare, and here I am starving to death! I will set out and go back to my father and say to him: 'Father, I have sinned against heaven and against you. I am no longer worthy to be called your son; make me like one of your hired servants'." So he got up and went to his father.

But while he was still a long way off, his father saw him and was filled with compassion for him; he ran to his son, threw his arms around him and kissed him.

The son said to him, "Father, I have sinned against heaven and against you. I am no longer worthy to be called your son."

But the father said to his servants, "Quick! Bring the best robe and put it on him. Put a ring on his finger and sandals on his feet. Bring the fattened calf and kill it. Let's have a feast and celebrate; for this

son of mine was dead and is alive again; he was lost and is found."
So they began to celebrate.

Meanwhile, the older son was in the field. When he came near
the house, he heard music and dancing. So he called one of the
servants and asked him what was going on. "Your brother has
come, "he replied, "and your father has killed the fattened calf
because he has him back safe and sound."

The older brother became angry and refused to go in. So his father
went out and pleaded with him. But he answered his father, "Look!
All these years I've been slaving for you and never disobeyed your
orders. Yet you never gave me even a young goat so I could celebrate
with my friends. But when this son of yours who has squandered
your property with prostitutes comes home, you kill the fattened
calf for him!" "My son," the father said, "you are always with me,
and everything I have is yours. But we had to celebrate and be glad,
because this brother of yours was dead and is alive again; he was
lost and is found."

Luke 15:11-32 NIV.

The Prodigal Son left home and squandered all of his inheritance.
He took life for granted and lived for the moment and selfishly
burned his bridges. He avoided his father and closed the door on
that relationship. If you were to ask him about his relationship with
his father, he might say, "We don't talk anymore, and if he knew
the things that I have done, he would never love me." He would
probably state, "I don't need him because he was never there for
me. This is his fault."

Have we not said the same things in relation to God? Many of us have boldly rejected God as we said something like, "I don't believe in God because it doesn't make sense," or "What kind of God would allow me to suffer like this?" Many of us were taught that God is a man in a white robe taking tally of all the mistakes that we make. We believe that if we ignore God, he will leave us alone and let us live the way we want to live.

We find when we search our hearts for the truth about God that we are wrong about God and his intentions. God is like the father in the prodigal son story. He celebrates our return to him. The Bible says that the angels rejoice in heaven when one of God's children reaches out to him and comes home. When the Prodigal Son returned home to ask for help, he was probably scared that he would be rejected and punished. He was wrong.

His father did not punish him. He received him with open arms. He ran to meet his son halfway. He rejoiced over his son's return home and forgave and accepted him. He told his other son who righteously believed that his brother should not be forgiven, "rejoice because he was *lost and now he is found.*"

> In the same way, there is more joy in heaven over
> one lost sinner who repents and returns to God
> than over ninety-nine others who are righteous
> and haven't strayed away! (Luke 15:7 NLT)

My story is a story of being lost and then found. I squandered all that God instilled in me. I was hurting and scared and I wanted *freedom.* I returned to a forgiving and loving father, and he and the angels rejoiced.

I felt it was important to tell my story. This is not a biography, and I will not go into every aspect of my life and my addiction to drugs and alcohol. The point of telling my story is to give a brief background so you can see the troubles I faced and how I found my way out! I have been thinking about this book for years and have brainstormed key points of recovery from my perspective. There are so many things I have learned about myself and about recovery in my years of sobriety and self-searching.

Working as a substance abuse counselor has shown me that many clients share the same struggles. I never push my beliefs on them. I have, however, seen many come to the same conclusion I have. These clients have embraced forgiveness, worked to challenge their old beliefs, and focused on learning to live a selfless and God-directed life.

But each journey begins with one step. My parents, my family and those who helped me as a child did the best they could, and I don't hold any resentment toward them. I love them and will always treasure the good times. I want to show a bit about my life and how I made sense of the world. I want to say, I don't blame anyone for my addiction or my bad choices. I take responsibility for my life and don't want to come off as though I am blaming anyone. I think our stories play a part in who we become, but ultimately we have to take control and responsibility. I realize today that no one is perfect.

I was born in Warren Michigan on June 20, 1973. I don't like looking at pictures of me as a baby or as a toddler. It concerns me that I am never smiling in pictures as a young child. I don't want to jump to any conclusions, but it appears as if I am not a very happy child. If we develop our personality and sense of self-esteem growing up, then I started off on the wrong foot.

My parents did the best they could when I was growing up. Dad worked in factories, and from what I have heard was a heavy drinker. My mom appeared to suffer from depression. My parents were divorced when I was young, apparently because of my father's drinking. I remember living in a motel room when I was about five years old. My mother was apparently depressed because she attempted to take her life by taking some pills. My grandmother watched me and my brothers while my mother was in the hospital. I experienced feelings of hopelessness and fear. I was always so afraid. Sometimes I would cry because I was scared and felt as though something bad was going to happen. In some respects, I just wanted someone to show me that everything was going to be all right.

Upon coming home from the hospital my mother met my stepdad. My stepdad was a good guy, but as with everyone, he had his defects. I remember feeling as though he was going to hurt my mother out of anger. I was always so afraid of everything. I was very intimidated and afraid of my stepdad. Today he is a pastor and was an integral part of me finding my way back to the Lord.

I always felt as though my brothers and I were the black sheep of my extended family. My mother did not work and we had very little resources. My parents were divorced, and I felt like a charity case. I always felt as though my extended family blamed my brothers and me for my parents' failures. I felt as though I was to blame for every bad thing that happened to my parents.

I am not saying that things were always bad. I don't want to make the claim that my childhood was always terrible and full of tragedy. I just want to show that I gained a sense of who I was by what I witnessed as a child. I had low self-esteem growing up, and it extended into adulthood. Fear leads to feelings of hopelessness and low self-esteem.

When I was growing up, my father was verbally abusive and constantly screamed at me and my brothers. I remember a few times where my father would strike me, but I would not actually call that abuse. Once he grabbed me by the back of my hair and screamed at me. Again I felt scared and hopeless. Man, I was always so afraid. I felt like a failure and believed I was the cause of my parents' struggles. My mother would also yell and tell me all the things that were wrong with me. The message from them in my eyes was, "If you weren't here, I would be happy." The rest of my family did the same thing. When I was around my mother's family, they would tell me what a drunk my father was, and when I was around Dad's family, they would tell me how my mother had ruined his life. I felt caught in the middle and began to believe that I was a bad child.

I had the label "I am bad." I learned later that having the belief that I was bad was a core belief. Core beliefs are idea's that come from cognitive behavioral therapy and are something you believe about yourself. These core beliefs come from deep down in your soul or core. I felt as though I was a burden to my parents and my family and that their lives would have been better if I had not been born.

As I went through school, I began experiencing problems. I was put in special classes for children who were falling behind. In sixth grade I felt stupid as I was always the last child to complete my multiplication tables during the timed tests. I grew up with the core beliefs that I was not smart and that I was a burden. I moved in with a friend's family when I was about twelve years old and found that wherever I went I always felt just like I had with my own family. I did not feel wanted or loved by anyone. Everywhere I went I felt out of place. Even though I had a loving family, I always felt as though I didn't belong.

Again, I don't blame anyone from my past for my bad decisions. Today I embrace forgiveness. I know that everyone has problems and I know that the people in my life when I was growing up did not purposely mean to hurt me. Most wanted to help, and the rest did not pay attention to how I was feeling. We have to overcome those obstacles. I know my parents loved me, and we had a good relationship at the time of their deaths. My father was sober 9 years at the time of his death and transition into Heaven. I know they both believed in Jesus and we will meet again in Paradise.

I found my first love in the bottle when I was twelve years old. I had my first negative consequence caused by alcohol at the same age when I ended up in the hospital after overdosing on it. Apparently, my mother found me passed out and called 9-1-1. I had to have my stomach pumped and spent the night there. I took all the hospital socks from the drawer in my hospital room: I was going to show them, I thought. Tears fell from my eyes as my mother drove me home without saying a word. Maybe I cried because she did not seem to care.

I swore that I would never drink again, but the desire to escape from negative feelings overcame me, and within a week I was drunk again.

By the time I was in high school, I was drinking every weekend and started smoking marijuana. I did not have many friends, and that was okay with me because I felt I did not need that kind of pressure anyway. I joined the theater club and played sports. I was frustrated during a talk with my parents about how they did not want me to play football because I was too small. That was another core belief in the bank: "I am too small." I needed to prove to my parents that they were wrong, so I joined anyway. I would go against the biggest guys on the team to show my worth. After getting the wind knocked out of me, I would get up and go back for more. I was always too small, too dumb, too ugly, too short, too poor, and full of fear. I didn't play much because of my size and lack of commitment. In fact, the last day of football in my senior year, my coach told me I had a lot of talent but did not have the commitment. I tried to overcome my insecurities by pretending to be confident and arrogant. But it was a lie. I was scared to death, afraid of girls, and afraid that others would see the real me: bad, ugly, small, stupid, a burden. It was easier to be alone.

After high school, I joined the US Navy. I was so proud to be a part of something so special and important. The navy instilled in me that I should be proud to serve my country. The problem was that all the negative things I felt about myself corrupted and pushed out any positive messages the navy tried to give me.

After basic training the United States Navy sent me to schooling to become an electrician. In school I found acceptance through friends who drank like me. We began to drink every night in electrician school. I would take caffeine pills every day before class to counteract the effects of alcohol from the night before. Amazingly, I made it through school. You see, positive messages were being sent to me by teachers but I was not listening. I was getting good grades and getting the praises from instructors. Sometimes we deny the obvious in light of the things we have always believed about ourselves. For example, I was at the top of my class but did not even pay attention to that. I believed I was stupid and ugly and no good for a long time.

I went to San Diego, California, after my electrician schooling in the navy, and on the first day there I got drunk and could not find my way back to my ship. I drank every chance I got, and the navy began to notice. I began to wake up in the mornings sick as a dog. I began to get arrested. I began to get into fights. I began to unravel. The personnel on the ship responsible for identifying kids with problems had me evaluated for alcoholism and sent me to outpatient treatment. I did not take this treatment seriously as I was not even twenty-one yet. The ship's medical personnel were going to send me to inpatient treatment when outpatient did not work, but the navy decommissioned the ship and I got out of going.

I then moved to an aircraft carrier in North Island, California. Being on a ship with so many people was ideal because I could fly under the radar. At this time I made a crucial decision at a friend's apartment to experiment with methamphetamines. I became addicted to crystal meth and began to use it every weekend. I loved the way t it made me feel: happy and carefree. I also continued to drink alcohol on a daily basis.

In the summer of 1994, my ship went on a Western Pacific cruise, and I experienced all kinds of trouble in every port due to my drinking. I was brought back to the ship in an ambulance in Japan; I got into trouble in Korea and was not allowed to leave the ship for more than two hours in China. When we returned to the United States, the navy gave me the option to go to rehab or leave the military. I chose rehab and entered with the declaration that I needed help. I knew that my drinking was not normal and I had a problem with alcohol, and I desperately wanted assistance. I did well in treatment. I discussed my addictions and had a desire to stay sober. I could see the hope of having a good life in sobriety but did not realize how deep I was in. A week after rehab, I began to use crystal meth again.

The counselors in rehab told me that I would have to make some tough choices and find a new support system and new friends. I was young and believed I would be the exception to the rule and started hanging out with drug-using friends. I received my first driving under the influence conviction six months later, and the navy had had enough. They called my father and told him I had a drinking problem and they were going to have to discharge me before I hurt myself or someone else. My father told me later that he did not believe them because I did not have a drinking problem when I left. But within a few weeks of me coming home, my father realized I was a full-blown alcoholic. I drank to the point of being passed out every day, and close to a case of beer every night. I suffered from hangovers and did not show up to work half the time because I was sick. My father pleaded with me to stop drinking and threatened to kick me out of his house. He told me on several occasions, "I am not going to watch you drink yourself to death."

I made him feel as though he was the blame for my drinking, and I probably convinced myself that he was. I was unable to take responsibility for myself, and I was extremely selfish and out of control. I began to experience hallucinations and have seizures when I did not drink. I would try to only drink on the weekends because I did not want to lose my job and because I was tired and sick. I would stay sober from Monday until Thursday. I would then start to feel better around Thursday and decide to drink again, convincing myself I would somehow exhibit control.

I felt horrible. I was sick of being sick. I was alone. I was full of remorse and guilt, and I was depressed. I wanted to be set free from this madness but did not know how. I remember praying to God, "Please help me or take me out of this nightmare." Eventually he would give me the power and guidance to stay sober but I was not ready to surrender yet. Over the next several years I would try crack, opiates, Xanax, and anything I thought would make me feel good. I was overwhelmed and dominated by my failure. I would cry when intoxicated because I felt trapped. I was scared and hopeless. I was suffering and felt alone. The Prodigal Son was defeated and almost dead.

I hurt those around me. I was like a tornado that damaged everything I came in contact with. I reached to the God above and he broke the chains. I found freedom. I have gained a new perspective on life and feel peace and love. I don't feel bad about myself anymore, and I am a new man with a new name. God embraced me with open arms and gave me freedom. I cry tears of joy now; what a difference. I want you to have what I have: a free gift.

Did you hear that? Stop and listen: it is the sounds of angels singing when a child of God returns home.

I can never express the pain and fear I felt when I was in my addiction. I was locked up in the chains of my lifestyle. I prayed for help and wanted out. I was desperate for answers. I was lost and felt alone. No one could understand my pain.

I will never forget the spiritual experience I had toward the end of my drinking. I know now that the Lord was protecting me during my using and this experience was his first invitation to come back home. As I lay there sick in bed that day, I began to feel a sense of impending doom. I remember how scared I was. I started to cry and told myself, "I do not want to die." I lay there shaking and not being able to sleep. I remember the room lighting up really bright, and I envisioned a white glow that I believe was an angel in the left corner of the room. The angel said to me, "You are going to be all right." I felt a sense of peace and calm that I had never experienced before. I began to weep uncontrollably. I did not stay sober that day, but I did start to attend recovery meetings within a few weeks. I believe I took the first step toward my journey home that day. Today I understand that peace is an important aspect of recovery.

I began to attend recovery meetings in 1997 and began to learn about sobriety. I would attend ten meetings a week in those days. I accepted the spiritual side of recovery without hesitation. I worked on the steps of recovery and began to discover and grow. I learned that I operated on low self-esteem, fear, and resentments and that I was extremely selfish.

I stayed sober for the first few years as a result of attending recovery meetings, but I felt depressed and knew something was missing. I never knew true peace in those early years of sobriety. I stayed sober but had no purpose. I embraced life in sobriety because I had no choice. I still dealt with low self-esteem early in sobriety but avoided alcohol and drugs because I did not want to die. I still felt hopeless. I could not find peace, and I desperately wanted to be happy. I wanted to have a life and knew I could not do that while drinking. I used alcohol and drugs because I could not cope with life. I could not tolerate the world I lived in. I used to think that it was a miracle that I stayed sober while dealing with those negative feelings. Now I realize that God was keeping me sober and knew that eventually I would find the answer. Today I have found it and have been given purpose. Life without purpose is not worth living.

In 2003 I found the real answer to my prayers. That is when I found true freedom.

In 2000 my son was born. I separated from his mother, and it was devastating. I was sober but I was miserable. I was full of guilt and remorse for not being there for my son. I thought about suicide constantly for three years and did not know what to do or where to turn. I was attending recovery meetings but did not share with the other group members how I was feeling. I wanted relief from my emotional pain but didn't know how to get it and focused on death.

In 2003 I went to talk to my stepfather, who had changed his life years earlier and was now a pastor. I told him that I wanted to kill myself and I did not know what to do about it. He asked me if I believed in God, and I told him that I did. He then asked me if I believed that Jesus was God, and I told him I did not know. I grew up Catholic, so I understood the premise that Jesus was God in the flesh, but I never really embraced the teachings or totally understood them. We discussed the Bible, and I grilled him on all the reasons that I felt the Bible was wrong. I told him it was written by men. He was patient and told me that the Bible was inspired by God and that God worked through his people to write it. He told me that if I looked at the evidence I would see that the Bible is the word of God and that Jesus was God. He explained to me about Saul's conversion into Paul and how it would make no sense for a man who was killing Christians to turn and become one of the most prominent Christians of his day without intervention from the hand of God. This made sense to me.

I believe this was my second invitation. A few nights later I had another spiritual experience. I felt the sunlight of the spirit come over me, and I began to cry uncontrollably. I realized I was wrong and that I had rejected the Father. I asked Jesus to forgive me, and I invited him into my life. He received me that night with open arms. Like the Prodigal Son, my Father met me with open arms, and the heavens celebrated over its lost son now returned.

I had gone to church as a child believing that I knew God. Instead, I knew *of* God but did not *know* God. I began that day to develop a personal relationship with my Lord Jesus Christ. I was dying of alcoholism and drug addiction, and the Lord had seen me through. He knew that someday I would come to him. God has given me the ability to stay sober and find peace of mind. I have worked through guilt, shame, anger, resentments, and low self-esteem and have found peace. God has helped me through college, and I have received a master's degree in Counseling. I have done things that I never thought possible. I have children who I love very much. I have a great wife who puts up with my nonsense. I have wonderful support from family and friends who love me. I have purpose. I don't want to die anymore.

I know that many people struggle with the concept of God. Some embrace their relationship with the Lord freely and without reservations. Some are more cautious and are not sure. There are those who refuse God and are bitterly aggressive when it comes to the topic of him. I hope you will read this book with an open mind. Jesus set me free. I can only offer you my story of newfound freedom. I feel peace today, and my relationship with God is the most important aspect of my life. I am a changed man. The old Greg is washed away and is no more. I have been given a new identity in Christ. I have struggled and stumbled over the past sixteen years. I learn from every mistake. But a relationship with God is not about perfection; it is about growth. I have been on a sixteen-year journey, and I have not had a drink of alcohol in over thirteen years. I ran into some trouble three years ago with painkillers as a result of surgery, and I learned a lot from that experience and overcame it through the power of Christ. He overcame the world to give me power to do the same.

The rest of this book focuses on how I gained freedom and peace and a few of the key points to my recovery. Changing your life takes time and work.

Prayer

Lord, thank you for a changed life. Help me reach others so that they can experience the peace and serenity you have provided. Help me reach those in need.

······································

CHAPTER 2

Why Should I Quit?

······································

Therefore, if the Son makes you free, you shall be free indeed.

—John 8:36 NKJV

I wanted to write this book so I could reach those lost in addiction. I believe that some will embrace change and others will set the book down only to pick it up in the future. It is my hope they will read the whole book and then make a decision.

This chapter is designed to help those who are not sure they need to quit. If you know you have a problem and are just reading this book to increase your knowledge about spirituality, that is awesome. I want to help those who know they have a problem and those who are unsure alike. I am sure that the God part of this book scares some away. I beg you to have an open mind

So then, why quit?

My clients will tell you that I do not force my opinion on anyone. I ask clients to look within themselves and figure out if they need to make a change. Recovery is an inside job, and a personal decision must be made to undertake it. We have to get a good look at the problem, and being honest with ourselves is the key. We usually know that we have a problem but are unwilling to do something about it. Most of us feel hopeless to change and find it is easier to ignore the obvious. Fear of change can be an issue. Usually other people see a problem before we do.

For example, I knew I was an alcoholic and was desperate for escape. I did not need anyone to convince me that I had a problem. I just needed them to offer me a solution. I understand the fear.

The first step in the process of recovery is to identify the problem. Sometimes we are not aware that there is a problem or we try to minimize it. In my case, those around me realized I had a problem way before I was ready to admit it and do something about it. I would get irritated if anyone tried to confront me or tell me what to do. Maybe someone in your life is asking you to read this book because they are trying to help you and are worried about you. Again, have an open mind and realize that fear is the enemy. Fear of change has destroyed more addicts than anything else.

My clients always ask me the question, "How do I know if I am an alcoholic or addict?" My answer tends to shock them. I tell them, "I don't care if you call yourself an alcoholic or addict. I don't care about labels." Labels cause us to compare our drug use against the drug use of others. Most of the time, a question like that is designed to disqualify: if I don't use as much as he does, then I don't have a problem. We compare ourselves to others in order to disqualify ourselves as doing the same things they do so that we can continue what we are doing. The only question you need to ask is this: "Is my use of drugs and/or alcohol causing negative things in my life or negative things in the life of those around me, and do I desire to change that behavior?" We don't need to be homeless drug addicts living on the streets to make a change.

I ask clients to identify the negative consequences of continued use versus the positive aspects of living sober. If our drug and alcohol use is causing consequences for us and others, then we may have to change those behaviors. No one's use is exactly the same. Some have gone to prison for their use, and some are just tired of hurting the feelings of their spouses and children. Some experience severe consequences, and some have not yet had enough consequences. So what point do we make the choice to change?

Making the choice to stay sober is a personal decision. I know that many loved ones hope the addicts and alcoholics in their lives will change before they are ready.

Accepting that we have a problem is the starting point. Remember, fear is the enemy. Many people who struggle with addiction cannot find their way out. Some experience setback after setback and continue to use despite the thought that they should change. Even addicts and alcoholics who want to stop aren't always successful. Others want to find a solution to their problem, but can't seem to make any progress. They quit for a period of time but always end up back into their drug of choice. They make plans to get things right but can never stay committed to the process. They suffer from guilt, shame, and remorse because they don't want to suffer anymore. They attempt to block out the reality of their situations and convince themselves that things will be better tomorrow. Well, tomorrow never comes.

We have to take a hard look at our use and its consequences. It may help to write down all the negative things that have happened to us and to others as a result of our addiction. We may want to make a list of the reasons we want to quit using. I have my clients write this type of list. One of the hardest things for an addict to do is to look at how his or her use is affecting others. We live in a world dominated by selfishness. We cannot see past our immediate experiences, and we block out the negative aspects of use so that we can go on doing what we want. We have to have the courage to look at our problem without fear or reservation. A good honest look at oneself is just what the doctor ordered. In my case, for example, I didn't want to think that there was something wrong with me, and I was afraid of a self-searching. What I really wanted was for everyone to leave me alone.

The idea that we will somehow find a way to beat the game is the fantasy of everyone struggling with substance use. Some may spend a lifetime trying to figure out different ways to keep using or use "less harmlessly." We switch brands and drugs and try and find ways to keep getting high without quitting completely. I believe in abstinence. I don't believe in controlled using. One cannot be partly free.

The bottom line is that we need to take a good honest look at our lives and decide how we want to live. Do we accept the life we are living, or do we want something different? Denial destroys. Denial is a way to block out the stress and anxiety of a situation we find unbearable or unacceptable. When we deny the truth about our situation, we cannot change it, and our fear of change will destroy us. We cannot be afraid to look at the truth, and we have to break through our desire for complacency in order to find our way out.

Some may not be able to be honest and will go on using to a bitter end. A life full of pain and sadness awaits them. Yes, they may feel comfort with a few drinks or an injection of heroin, but they will never know true peace and will miss out on all life has to offer. It breaks my heart every time I hear a story of a young person overdosing on a drug or an elderly man dying all alone with his bottle. Life has so much more for us, and it takes courage to embrace change. Are you willing to step out in faith and try something new, or do you want to block out your situation as best you can and let life pass you by?

If you have a problem, you may be able to benefit from my story of redemption. I tell my clients to take what they can use to help their recovery. I found freedom, and I believe deep in my heart that you can have it too. We start off with a seed of hope, and we allow it to grow into full-blown recovery.

I have known many people who could not make the decision to stay sober. I have seen them struggle with the decision to make serious changes in their lives. Many people can see the benefits of sobriety but are unwilling to dream of a life free of drugs and alcohol.

The prospect of a life like that is too much for many to comprehend. Some have lost jobs and have found themselves in the emergency room on many occasions. Some have faced years in prison and the reality that their drug of choice might someday cost them their lives. It is amazing to me when I hear addicts discuss how their use has cost them so much and how they have hurt others around them only to joke about and glorify drugs and alcohol a few days later. I have had clients tell me how they were brought back to life by medical staff only to shove a needle in their arm the next day. I have heard of men and women who have lost their families because of drinking alcohol only to state that they may drink again when things get back on track in their lives.

We all have different stories, but we have to focus on the reality of the situation. We cannot lie to ourselves anymore. We have to get to the point where we look in the mirror and say, "Nothing good can come out of my use anymore, and I am willing to do whatever it takes to have a new life. I am willing take a step of faith in order to have peace and freedom."

Many will also try to minimize their use. I have known men and women who attended church every Sunday and attempted to convince everyone else that they had it together, only to go home and drink a twelve-pack of beer in isolation in front of the television. These men and women would tell you that they work without missing time. They pay their bills and have a savings account. What they cannot see is the subtle consequences of such use. We have to accept that using drugs and alcohol is against the will of God and his plan for our lives. We have to be honest about the consequences of our use.

We have a chance to experience life the way that life was meant to be lived. We have to believe that our lives can be different. But letting go of everything we know and trying something new is not an easy prospect. Some will be deep in addiction and make it out. Some will be at the brink of disaster and recover. Some will come to realize that their use is causing problems even if it isn't obvious and will fight for sobriety. Some will not make it out at all and will spend the rest of their days living a lie.

I can tell you that things can get better and you can reach your potential by coming into fellowship with Jesus. He can help us live normal lives. Life will knock us down, it will be tough, we will fall, but with Jesus we will always overcome.

When I decided to quit, I was at the point of self-destruction, and I owed it to myself and my family to give something else a try. I have experienced success and failure in sobriety. I have experienced peace and sadness. I gained power through my newfound friend. I found Jesus! I did not believe I would ever be able to stop drinking and drugging. I was hopeless and helpless, and I had no reason to think things would change. I was wrong. The Lord has given me freedom, and all I had to do was accept him into my life. Doing so is a personal decision, and each of us has to make it. Many will be set free by the power of God, and many will not accept his gift. What will you do?

As for me, I don't want to hurt others anymore, and I don't want to feel the pain of running away from my problems and my life. I don't want to live like an ostrich with my head buried in the sand. I don't want my family to look at my gravesite and wish they could have said something to save my life. I don't want to experience the pain and the sadness my addiction brought. I want to live free. I want to be a good example for my children. I want others to look at my life as a story of redemption and not a story of desperation. I know that someone was praying for me when I was using, and I am praying for you. I want the chains of addiction to be broken for everyone. I know God is tired of his children suffering and dying too young. The pain on the faces of our loved ones is too much to bear. We owe it to ourselves to try something new.

If we turn to God, he will help us out. If we ask, we will receive. If we allow him to teach us and help us to grow, we will be free. I had just a small seed of faith, and I allowed Jesus to do the rest. I believe in the power of God. I believe he put me down here to have life in abundance, and I choose not to spend it hiding anymore. Drugs and alcohol give us a false sense of peace. It is a lie. I had never experienced true peace and purpose until I asked and embraced a relationship with my Creator. I know freedom and happiness. He gives me the strength to face life on life's terms. I cannot stay sober without his power and strength. I know today that my relationship with God is the most important thing in my life.

The rest of the book is focused on growing in the likeness of the creator. As we work through the next chapters, we will find new ways to relate to our Lord. We will learn how to find peace and embrace a new life. Godly men in the Bible like Abram were given new life and a new name. Abram became Abraham and he was born anew. I have been born anew, and I have worked to rid myself of the stumbling blocks that can come between me and my power.

Prayer

Lord, I pray that many will come to find your new way of life. That I will have the courage to trust in you and believe that you can release me from my chains. I pray, dear Lord, that many will read this information and be able to take an honest look at their lives and desire change. We know that you are the breaker of chains and the author of new life. Give me a new name, Lord, as I am reborn in your likeness. In Jesus' name. I pray. Amen.

CHAPTER 3

Finding Peace

Peace I leave with you, my peace I give to you; not as the world gives do I give to you. Let not your heart be troubled, neither let it be afraid.

—John 14:27 NKJV

I had a client in group therapy ask me to define peace. So I did what any good counselor does and asked the group to define it. Clients stated things like: feeling good, feeling content, feeling quiet inside, feeling safe, and feeling as though there is nothing to worry about.

I agreed with all their definitions, but I would expand on them to define peace as a feeling of awe and power coupled with the sense that nothing can harm us in God's hands. I have felt peace that cannot be expressed, or what Christians call the movement of the Holy Spirit of God. Sometimes when I am in church and we are praising God, I feel so moved and free that I tear up. I feel forgiven and loved.

One of the most important aspects of my recovery is my need to have peace and serenity. I don't like to feel uncomfortable or worried. I don't like to be stressed out, and I certainly don't like to be upset. I drank and used drugs essentially because I didn't feel good and wanted to feel better. It was a way to eliminate negative emotions and to increase positive emotions. It is important to note that I also drank and used drugs while experiencing positive emotions. Today, I recognize my negative internal triggers for using drugs and alcohol include negative emotions that make me feel uncomfortable like worry, anger, frustration, anxiety, fear, guilt, shame, and remorse.

When I feel weak and uncomfortable, I know how to temporarily feel better. I know the short-term feelings of euphoria that can be attained by taking a few drinks or some drugs. I know today that I am vulnerable to using when I am not feeling right. I am a runner by nature. I now realize that I used to run and hide in alcohol and drugs. However, it is important to understand that internal triggers to use may also include positive emotions like feeling motivated, excited, and energetic. (I'll talk more about triggers later.).

It was very difficult for me to attain sobriety at first because I did not have any peace. I was holding on to sobriety for dear life and not feeling very good

Using drugs and alcohol gave me a momentary sense that everything was going to be all right. When I was stressed, alcohol and drugs relaxed me. When I was angry, they calmed me down. When I was feeling worried or lonely, I would get drunk. I felt a false sense of peace and confidence when I was high. The problem arose when I would come down or sober up. When sober, I would feel the opposite of these things. I would feel irritable, angry, upset, frustrated, depressed, lonely, stressed, worried, afraid, and bored. I could not stay sober because I could not deal with negative emotions. Now I realize that drugs and alcohol offered a temporary fix to a bigger problem: not feeling good about who I was.

Using was a façade: I only thought I was dealing with life. I had this illusion when I was high that life was all right and there were no problems. But I could only run for so long before the drugs and alcohol stopped working. I would drink and get high and feel terrible when I came down or sobered up. I would cry for no reason. I would punch stops signs, and hurting myself felt good.

I was full of fear, and I lost all control over how much I would consume. In the end, I was trying to control something that was completely out of control. I needed to find another way.

When I am uncomfortable today, I know this is a dangerous place for me. I can always use feeling bad as an excuse to give up and run to the bottle. When dealing with life's worries and frustrations, I sometimes get a desire to escape and to feel good. At these vulnerable moments, I remember how good the first few drinks felt, and I block out all the negative aspects of using.

But for me to drink or use is to lose. I don't want to lose all I have gained in sobriety. I don't want to end up back in my addiction. Today my sobriety is dependent on feeling comfortable and having peace of mind. I have learned to monitor my emotions and become aware of how I am feeling at any given time. I have to be vigilant, and my spiritual life becomes the battlefield for my struggles against negative emotions.

Obtaining Peace

My Creator does not desire for me to be enslaved to substances. I believe Jesus was looking down on me all those years, feeling pity and sadness as he watched me killing myself. I know he protected me in times of trouble. I believe he kept me safe because he had a plan for my life. He has a plan for all of us. He wants us to trust him and accept him.

I have found that a belief in Jesus offers me refuge when I'm dealing with these negative emotions. I have felt the presence of God and have experienced peace through trust in him and surrender. I fall down on my knees and ask God to clear the path that leads to his throne. I have learned to forgive myself and others, to face my fears, and release control. I allow God to guide me and choose to embrace his will and his word: the Bible. I feel peace when I trust that God has forgiven me. I know what it is like to be completely sober and feel complete tranquility. I have the faith that everything is going to be all right. When I am close to my Creator, I feel comfortable in my skin, and I have the power to stay sober. I have never experienced anything like it in my life. I get on my knees and pray and refuse to get up until I feel the presence of God. I always believed the word "surrender" meant losing control of my life. I believed I would lose my sense of independence if I turned my life over to God. I was completely wrong. I have freedom when trusting in God and allowing him to clean out every corner of my life. I have allowed Jesus to mold me into who he wants me to be. I found a purpose in life that brings peace and power.

I am a work in progress, and some days are better than others. I trust God to show me how to live, and I allow him to guide me. I am miserable when I allow my will to take over and selfishness kicks in. But I feel peace when I am in the will of God, and lose my peace whenever I start to worry about the world and try to force my will into it. I do not always feel at peace, but I never feel the desire to run anymore. I have confidence in my Creator, and I am absolutely positive that he will see me through any trouble. I stand firm in faith.

Sobriety is not an easy choice for some, and it wasn't for me. I could not let go of the past long enough to grasp the future. I was caught between wanting to be free and wanting to be worldly. But I cannot live as many others do in this world. I must embrace God as the solution to my problems. It is hard to change. It takes courage to trust what you cannot see. Christians believe in the power of God because we have seen it save others. We crack the door of faith so that Jesus can show himself. We realize that the Lord will always reveal himself to those who ask of him. Jesus always teaches me something in the storms and I come out better on the other side. I have felt the presence of God and could never describe it if I had too. Like the Prodigal Son, I returned home and found my father waiting to anoint me with his blessings and love. Today I have peace, and today I am free because he broke the chains that held me captive.

It is scary to me how many people are walking through life without purpose and peace.

I walked into a group therapy session one day and sat down. My clients all waited for me to tell them what the topic of the day was going to be. We discuss many things in group, and they usually can relate with most topics. On this day, I walked up to the whiteboard and wrote the word *peace*. I sat back down and listened to what the group members had to say. I heard some say that they were at peace when they were using alcohol and drugs. Some said they felt at peace when they were listening to music. Several of the group members stated that they had never once in their lives felt at peace. As one client put it, "I have never had peace. Peace is not a reality for me, and I wouldn't even know how to describe it."

I remember thinking that I used to feel that way. I remembered when I was using drugs and alcohol and had no peace in my life. I remember my early years in sobriety when I was always tense and agitated. I did not know what peace was until I became reunited with my maker.

Lesson Learned

One morning I was on my knees next to my bed praying. My mind kept racing, and I could not focus. I had a list of things I wanted God to do for me. I realized then that even in the midst of a prayer I did not have peace. I knelt there and thought, *I am going to clear my mind and ask the spirit of God to come in.*

It seemed as though half an hour went by, but it was probably only a few minutes. Suddenly, a feeling of euphoria came over me. I felt free and heard the quiet of my thoughts. I felt the peace of God that day.

I realize that sometimes God wants me to be quiet and listen. I am always talking. So I attempt to quiet my mind and allow God to fill me with his spirit. I have never taken a drug that compared to that feeling of peace when listening to the voice of God.

Every morning when I wake up I turn on Christian music. I find it to be uplifting, and it puts me into the spirit of God. I also feel peace and power when I am at church on Sundays. I feel it when I look into my children's eyes and they smile. I cry tears of joy on the way to work listening to songs about God and praying for his spirit to guide me. I have known peace and power like never before. I walk with God and know he has a plan for me. His plan is a good plan. It is a plan to help others and be of service to this world. I know his mission for me is to bring others the knowledge of his saving grace. I have no doubt in the existence of God. I believe in God not because I read about him in a book, but because I have experienced him by asking. Remember, all we have to do is ask and we shall receive. I believe everyone has access to the throne of God.

Christians ask his son into our lives. Everyone who wants freedom has to ask Jesus into their lives. He listens to their prayers and gives them strength and power. We do not make demands of God but trust that he knows what is best for our lives. We have faith that he can give us the power to stay sober and succeed. I have never found meaning in life outside the will of God. I want to be a good father today. I want to be a good husband, brother, leader, and counselor. I know that is what God wants for me.

I hope that you can have what I have. It is more precious than gold or silver. It is the healing power of Jesus. My heart breaks for those who have never known peace; what a shame. I have the ability today to feel for others. I have the ability to want good things for complete strangers. I have love in my heart for God's children. I will pray that all who read this book and ask Jesus into their hearts find peace. A life without peace is not worth living.

We find it in Christ.

Prayer

Lord, help me to stay close to you. Help me to remember that you are still in charge and have my best interests in hand. I trust in you, Lord, for you have seen me through the storms and have strengthened me in my times of sorrow. I ask of you to show me peace and give me serenity. Allow me to feel your presence in all I do. In your son Jesus' name, I pray. Amen.

CHAPTER 4

Anger, Resentment, and Forgiveness

And, "Don't sin by letting anger control you. Don't let the sun go down while you are still angry."

—Ephesians 4:26 NLT

I like to have peace and serenity in my life. I realized a long time ago that my sobriety is directly related to my peace of mind and how I feel in the world. Don't get me wrong, I am not weak enough to run to drugs and alcohol at the first sign of trouble. However, I won't suffer long before I will start to think about escape. I realize the quickest way for me to lose footing and my peace of mind is to get angry. This may not apply to everyone, but my anger has always been a problem.

Anger

Whenever anyone comes into conflict with my desires or my will, I am quick to anger. I told my clients this story of when I was in the gym the other day: I was working out, and every time I dropped the weights, a woman mumbled under her breath. I hate when people whisper, and it drove me nuts. I tried to ignore it, but every time I dropped the weights to the ground, she started making little comments. She said to her friend, "Today must be 'drop as much weight as you can' day."

I was getting irritated. My clients have told me that they can tell when this happens because my face starts to turn red. Well, my face was getting beet-red at those comments. I thought, *How dare you make comments about me? Do you think you can just say whatever you want about me while I sit here and take it?* I had several anger-causing thoughts running around my head, and I was starting to get angry. I knew that if I did not adjust my thinking immediately, there was going to be a problem. I understood at that moment that I needed to focus on my negative thoughts and change them. If I hadn't, I would have probably told the woman off, or at least said something rude to her.

You might say, "Who cares? I would have told her what I thought." Well, I will tell you this: I have come to understand a few things about anger over the years. First, my negative behaviors like anger cause me guilt, and guilt is another trigger for me to get drunk. Second, I lose my peace of mind when I am angry.

So, I took a deep breath and told myself not to let others bother me. I prayed for God to help me withhold judgment and forgive her. I smiled at her and her friend and walked away. I have to admit I was angry for a while, and it took time for it to pass. Again, if I had gone off on this woman and said what I was thinking, doing so could have caused me remorse and guilt. I would have allowed her to take control over my thoughts and my life and would have had a great excuse to drink.

Let me clarify something: anger in itself is not always bad. Anger protects us from harm. We get angry when we view something as a threat. Anger signifies that we are in danger. It is a natural emotion. If used in the right way, anger can be positive, as an indicator that something is bothering us and needs to be addressed. For example, if I get angry at myself for relapsing, then I can use that anger as motivation to change. If my wife has cheated on me four times and that is causing me to relapse, then I can use that anger to make the choice to leave her and make positive changes in my life that can help me stay sober. I use anger to help me to make changes.

The problem arises when we use anger ineffectively. Instead of leaving my wife and getting sober, for example, I could lose my peace of mind and go out and get drunk. I don't know how many times I used anger in the past as an excuse to use and get high. When I experienced anger, I did not use it to grow. Rather, I used it to feel sorry for myself and throw myself in victim mode. I allowed it to defeat me.

Let me explain: when I handle anger ineffectively, I tend to have thoughts—in the case of the woman at the gym, for example—such as, *How dare they do that to me? Who do they think they are? No one does that to me! They must think I am weak and won't protect myself! I will show them that no one does that to me!* These negative thoughts have one thing in common: they make me feel weak and like a victim. In the case of the woman at the gym the negative thoughts caused me to feel bad about myself. We need to learn to deal with our thoughts more effectively, or we run the risk of allowing others to control us.

My clients often respond to this advice with, "You are crazy! No one can stop themselves from getting angry."

I tell them, "We can get angry, but we need to take control of it and learn to get rid of it."

We take control of anger by recognizing the thoughts and then focusing on how to let them go or change them. In the gym, I recognized that the woman's words were causing me anxiety, which I saw as a threat, so I focused on my thoughts, took control of them, concentrated on changing them, and moved on. I eventually forgave her and forgot about it. I remained free of resentment and felt peace and serenity.

We need to look at our own anger. It may help to put a situation on paper and look how our anger is being used (see the anger challenge at the end of the chapter). If I get angry and tell myself I deserve to be, then I can use my anger to justify some bad behaviors and feelings.

Justified or unjustified, anger can be used to wrongly defend drinking, drugging, fighting, being rude, being controlling, being judgmental, being argumentative, isolated, or frustrated, feeling depressed, anxious, or sorry for ourselves, and many more negative things. Anger gets out of control then, and we become constantly in conflict with others.

We all know people who are continuously angry. They complain they are being taken advantage of and tend to constantly focus on others. They use their anger to blame other people and to avoid taking responsibility for their lives.

People who struggle to take responsibility for their thoughts and emotions are prone to anger. For example, I was a person who blamed everyone else for my problems and could not take responsibility for myself or my actions. I always played the blame game and kept myself in victim mode. Today, I don't like and am not comfortable when feeling angry and frustrated. Rather, I want to live in peace and to experience serenity. I learn from my anger.

I know now I will never be free from anger, but I make progress and that is okay with me. I realize it is a natural reaction to a real or perceived threat. Today, I try to limit anger and get rid of it as soon as it rears its ugly head. I focus on the thoughts and try to work through them. I take responsibility for them and try to forgive myself and others.

It takes practice to identify the thoughts that cause us anger. The anger challenge at the end of the chapter can help with that. In it, we look at a time when we were angry and try to remember the thought that came before the feeling. The things we believe about ourselves and the world affect the way we think. Negative feelings come from negative thoughts, which come from negative beliefs. Completing the worksheet at the end of this chapter will help you recognize and work through these. Christians need to avoid anger because it affects our relationship with God and his power in our lives. Our Lord forgave us and commands us to live in the spirit of forgiveness.

Resentment

When anger turns into resentment, it is even worse. My definition of resentment is a deep-rooted anger that is not easily let go.

I have had some of these resentments in my life, and I still struggle with some deep-seated anger. I have had loved ones steal from me, lie to me, and cheat me out of my inheritance. I have struggled to forgive them. Ultimately, I realized those deep-seated resentments were toxic to my recovery.

There is a saying that resentment is like taking poison and expecting the other party to die. I have to learn to relinquish those resentments because those resentments invade my space. They invade my sleep and take up my precious time. They are like chains that bind me. Resentment controls my thoughts and my emotions. I realize today that I can use resentments to provide a false sense of security. I can convince myself that I have been hurt by others and can feel sorry for myself and make excuses for my poor actions and choices. Resentments keep me from feeling free, lower my self-worth, and keep me feeling depressed and afraid. I can also take my anger and resentments and turn them inward and allow them to turn into anger against myself. I can then feel like a victim and feel sorry for myself, and feeling sorry for ourselves is an easy way to avoid taking responsibility.

At first self-pity feels nice and warm, but after a while it starts to stink. We cannot take poison anymore. We need to realize that holding resentment blocks us off from God and his desire for our lives. We should ask the Lord to help us be rid of anger and resentment because nothing will destroy an addict or alcoholic faster than holding on to it. If we have resentments, we feel justified to take a drink. Resentments cause victim mentality, and this makes it impossible for us to take control.

Today I have to take responsibility for my behaviors and quickly release anger and resentment. During a Bible study last year, I went on my knees before God and prayed for the family member who stole from me. I asked Jesus to take away my anger and resentment and set me free. I was tired of living in bondage to that hurt. It was occupying too much of my time and energy, and I needed to let it go. Instead, I asked Jesus to give this family member all the things I wanted in life for myself. I asked that this person be saved and forgiven. I am not in bondage to that resentment anymore.

Forgiveness

And if he sins against you seven times in the day, and turns to you seven times, saying, "I repent," you must forgive him.

—Luke 17:4 ESV

If we confess our sins, he is faithful and just to forgive us our sins and to cleanse us from all unrighteousness.

—1 John 1:9 NKJV

Jesus came down to earth so he could die for our sins. He released me from my debt and took my punishment. He died and saved me. He offered to me what I did not deserve. That is what forgiveness is. Forgiveness is erasing the debt owed to us without reservation and payback.

When I forgive someone, I am letting his or her offense go without reservation. I am saying, that he or she doesn't not need to pay for that debt anymore and that I release it. When I forgive someone, I set myself free from the control the offense he or she caused me has over my life. Anger and resentment invade our spaces and have control over us. I don't know about you, but I don't like to be controlled. I like to have peace of mind, and I like to feel at ease. I realize that anger and resentment block me off from God's will. I know that the Lord does not want me living in judgment of others. Jesus said that we are to forgive those who trespass against us as our Father forgives us for our trespasses. We need to let go of our anger and resentment, and we pray that God gives us the strength to forgive.

Forgiveness is very difficult. At one point in my life, I could never forgive others because it felt as though doing so would justify their actions. I would think, *Why should they be set free for that wrong? They do not deserve to be set free.* I believed they should pay for what they did and forgiving them would be like letting them think their actions were no big deal. But if God could send his son down here to die for my sins, then I should be able to forgive a family member who decided to steal from me. I realize that when I set that person free, I really set myself free. I try not to be in bondage of others' bad behavior. I don't want to pay for their mistakes, so if I hold resentment, I allow them to control me. Today, I want peace and I strive to feel good. I release the people who wrong me because that is what God has asked me to do. It is not easy, but it is necessary.

Prayer

Lord, help me to leave the judgment of others to you. Help me to forgive those who have offended me and allow me to be free from their control. I pray that I may experience peace in your light and find truth in your Word. Help me to recognize and deal with my anger effectively. Give me a spirit of forgiveness. Amen.

Anger Challenge

Situation:

Thought and Feeling:

Belief:

What action would you take with this type of thinking?:

Different thought:

Different feeling:

Different action:

Anger Challenge (My Example)

Situation: Women making comments about me at gym.

Thought and Feeling: Angry. How dare she talk to me that way?

Belief: People don't confront me. I am weak if I don't say something. Rude people deserve to be confronted.

What I would normally do: Tell her off and maybe use the whole situation as an excuse to get drunk.

Different thought: I am not going to let her control me.

Different action: Pray for her and move on.

Different feeling: Peace.

I need to learn to think about situations differently so I feel different and act differently. When using the anger challenge, I can see how my anger is causing problems. I can use it in every situation that causes anger.

CHAPTER 5

Finding Self-Worth

Let me start by telling you about a person I will call "Shorty" for confidentiality reasons. Shorty was a client in a rehab center I worked at who was a mean and nasty individual. Clients and staff tried to stay clear of Shorty because of his negative attitude. He was likely to go off at any moment. He had a violent past and was not afraid of confrontation. In fact, he seemed to operate on it. Most people wanted Shorty out of the program as soon as possible.

Well, Shorty was put on my case load, and I was enthused. During our first session, he began to get irritated and then angry. He started to talk about how everyone got on his nerves and how his friend, who was a drug dealer, just got killed over the weekend. Shorty discussed how he wanted to exact revenge on the people who killed his friend. I found it hard to calm him down.

I asked Shorty why other people aggravated him so much. He stated that he did not know; he just didn't like people and others could not be trusted. I asked him to tell me about a situation where he experienced anger. He talked about one time when a female client in the facility got in his face and ticked him off. I asked him to think about what thoughts led up to his anger in that situation. He had no idea what I was talking about, so I asked him what thoughts came before he decided to go off on her.

He said, "I guess I was thinking that she should mind her own business and stay out of mine."

I asked him what it meant to have someone in your business. Again, he seemed confused. He stated, "I don't like people getting in my business."

"Shorty," I said, "I want you to think about what message is being sent to you when others get into your business."

"I guess it means that they think they are better than me or think that they can control me," he said.

"So, when others judge you, it creates anger."

"I guess so," he replied.

"What does it mean to you when someone judges you?"

He thought for a minute. "That I am not as good as them or that they are better than me."

"Do you think they are better than you, or that you are not good enough?" I asked.

"I suppose I don't feel good enough," he said.

At this point, Shorty appeared calmer. I asked who in the past had told him he was not good enough. I think that question shocked him because he stared at me for a moment and began to tear up.

"My father," he said.

With tears in his eyes, he went on to tell how his father always put him down and made him feel like a failure. I cannot tell you what he said next because it was pretty vulgar. But after that, he said, "I never realized that I felt like I was not good enough."

Shorty came to the conclusion that he operated on the presumption that he was a bad person because that was what he believed about himself. His lack of self-worth created a huge problem for him. He was always in conflict with others and always felt as though he was being attacked. He believed what his father said and allowed that message to dominate his life.

I wish I had good news about Shorty, but after a few days he was kicked out of the program. Change is a process. I hope Shorty figures out what is hurting him and gains the power to change his life.

Shorty's negative beliefs affect how he views himself and others. In a sense, he has to learn to challenge his father's message. Shorty is not a bad person but a person who is operating on false beliefs.

Self-esteem is the way we view ourselves, and the image we have of ourselves may be good or bad. The way we view ourselves plays a major role in how we act, live, and feel, and what we feel about ourselves affects the way we view the world and its occupants. People with low self-esteem tend to have negative opinions of themselves and the world they live in.

We develop a sense of self by the messages we receive from our parents, our teachers, society, and those we come in contact with. We listen to messages from those around us, and we attempt to make sense of those messages. If we are told that we are not good enough and believe that, doing so will affect how we view the world and ourselves.

What we believe affects the way we think. In Shorty's case, he believed he was being judged. He held negative beliefs and reacted to others based on those beliefs. He was always thinking negatively because he believed negative things about himself and others.

We have to make a list on paper of our negative beliefs so we can get a good picture on how we operate. For example; Do we feel like failures? Do we believe others cannot be trusted, and why? Do we believe people tend to use us? Do we think people are liars? Do we feel judged? A counselor or therapist can help us to deal with these negative beliefs so we can function more effectively.

I have found that reading God's Word and living according to his will has removed many of these pitfalls for me. God has the power to help us through troubles, and he can give us the strength and peace to stand up to these negative beliefs. Learning to identify negative thoughts and negative beliefs takes time and effort. It also takes time to change the way we think and feel. We cannot be afraid to change. We need to realize that there is benefit in change. We want to experience peace and live life more effectively. We need to ask God to give us the strength to take a good hard look at ourselves and our motives. We have to decide that we want to live at a higher level, and we need to be willing to do whatever it takes to stay sober and feel at peace in sobriety. Again, we may need the help of a professional or at the very least a trusted friend who can assist us in seeing the truth behind our motives and beliefs.

Some of our beliefs have been ingrained in us since childhood, and they are not just going to vanish just because we are aware of them. We have to work to understand why we act and feel the way we do. In my case, I have always felt as though I was not smart enough or good enough. Because of this, I experienced a lot of stress in college. I did not think I was smart enough to earn a degree. In fact, I earned a master's degree with a 3.8 GPA and still felt stupid. I know, however, that I am smart, and the belief that I am stupid is false. I tell myself I am a good and compassionate counselor and that I have the ability to help others. I know I am a child of God and that I am worthy of love as a child of God. I realize that negative beliefs and thoughts steal away my mission. It takes time and energy to learn to feel good about ourselves, and we have to stay sober while doing so. When we get sober and start to grow, our lives get better, so we have to have the courage to face life. We have to have the strength to try something new. It takes time to change, but each journey begins with the first step. We must be patient. We will make progress and realize that we will never reach perfection.

So why is developing positive self-worth so important?

My low self-worth created my need to escape. I could not deal with life because I did not believe in myself and my ability to cope. I was sent negative messages as a child, so I believed that I was not good enough, I was too skinny and not smart enough. I believed I was a bad kid and that I could not measure up. As a result, I suffered from depression and anxiety and used alcohol and drugs to cope with a world I could not function in. As I began to drink and make bad choices, my self-worth decreased. The pain I caused others and the way I lived my life made me feel even worse. It was a vicious cycle. I was full of guilt, shame, remorse, fear, anxiety, stress, and depression. I felt worthless and truly believed I was a bad person, and I had to drink because I did not want to feel bad. As I've said before, I won't suffer long before I seek escape.

Many clients have told me that they relate to my living with low self-esteem. Many have used drugs or alcohol as a result of not feeling good about themselves. The guilt and the remorse of their lifestyle then created more using and a need to escape.

I had to develop a sense of positive self-worth in order to stay sober. I sought therapy to help me deal with the belief that I was not good enough, that I was a bad, unwanted boy. However, I don't want to blame my parents or anyone else for my problems; I was the one who put the bottle to my mouth and drank. I do not hold anyone responsible for my actions, and I have learned to deal with my low self-worth. I started to feel better about myself when I began the road to sobriety. I worked through some of the negative feelings I had toward myself and others. I learned to overcome my resentments and to forgive others. I also needed to forgive myself for all the mistakes I had made. I realized I am smart, loving, and generally a good person. I realize today that everyone is both good at times and bad at times. I learned to love myself and what it means to love others unconditionally. I learned that my God loves me and forgives me and that feeling bad and experiencing low self-worth is counterproductive. Low self-worth leads to relapse: when I feel bad, I leave myself in a position to make excuses for bad behaviors. I believe God wants me to feel good about myself. He wants me to help others and to be of service to him. He lifts me up when I feel down. He gives me strength when I feel weak. He lets me know that I am a good person. God loves me even when I make bad decisions.

We have to learn to send ourselves more positive messages and stop the negative self-talk. When we learn to identify negative thoughts, we can become aware of our thinking patterns. We need to practice turning negative thoughts into more realistic positive thoughts and to accept ourselves and our limitations.

The Bible says that all have sinned and fallen short of the glory of God. We must allow ourselves to get better. We have to believe in the power of forgiveness and love. We need to know that we can trust our God to help us through the valleys and storms. We must tell ourselves that our mistakes do not define who we are. We have to be ready to take firm action and overcome our past behaviors. We must also realize that those who may have sent us negative message are also imperfect and worthy of forgiveness. We have to break the chains of trauma so we can walk free in the sunlight of God. When we recognize low self-worth, we must immediately deny it and tell ourselves that we are not bad and that we live for a higher purpose in God, that we are loved because God is love. We have to believe our lives have meaning, and we must search for that meaning in Christ. If you believe that you are a failure and unworthy, you are lying to yourself. We all have purpose in this life, and that purpose is to live God's way.

Today I desire to be free, and I find freedom in God's love and acceptance. Christians pray and ask God to forgive us for our sins and to help us to forgive others. We need to believe that nothing good can come from feeling bad about ourselves. Our Father in heaven loves us and expects us to show the same love to others.

Prayer

Lord, help me to recognize when I am feeling bad about myself. Help me to forgive myself and others as you have forgiven. Show me how to live in your will and allow me to be free from the chains that bind me. Give me strength to accept the love you have shown me and help me to love others. In your son Jesus' name I pray. Amen.

CHAPTER 6

Overcoming Fear

For God had not given us the spirit of fear, but of power and love and of a sound mind.

—2 Timothy 1:7 NKJV

First let me say that fear is not always a bad thing. Fear is designed to protect us in the event of danger. If I am confronted by a big man with a crowbar in an alley, I might get a little worried. I teach my children they could get hurt if they run in the middle of the highway. When I am afraid, I have to look at the situation and decide what action to take. I can either run or fight. Fear in itself is not a bad thing. It becomes a problem when we cannot see it for what it is or when it controls our lives. When I talk about fear, I am talking about out-of-control fears that create internal and external difficulties. Fear tends to dominate and manipulate, and it can blind us to the truth. Fear keeps us from operating at full capacity, bankrupts us, and keeps us from taking control. It is at the root of many human difficulties. Fear causes stress, anxiety, anger, depression, low self-esteem, violence and many other forms of spiritual sickness. God asks us to have faith. Fear is the opposite of faith.

Fear is not something most of us believe is a problem. The acronym FEAR in recovery is either "forget everything and run," or "face everything and recover." Fear is one of the most devastating things that we can deal with, and it plays a role in anxiety, frustration, anger, jealousy, depression, worry, hatred, resentment, stomach ulcers, and feeling a need to escape. The effects of fear are great indeed. Peace and fear cannot coexist. Both touch every aspect of our lives.

We all experience fear. It may hide itself in anger and frustration, but it is there. I can trace back any uncomfortable feeling to fear. It is a subtle foe, in part because men and women are taught to "be strong" by ignoring it. In fact, I was taught this. My father taught me that if someone is going to hurt you, you strike first. He told me to quit being a baby and grow up. I told myself growing up that showing fear or talking about it would be a sign of weakness and others would think less of me. I was afraid of being judged.

Today, I don't like focusing on being afraid because it makes me feel weak and ashamed. I don't want to tell my wife or my kids that I am afraid because they are supposed to think that I am strong, tough, and a good provider. My son doesn't go to school and say, "My dad can bench-press 300 pounds, and he is a coward." (Yes, I can bench press 300 pounds—350 to be exact). People teach us to be strong and not to show weakness because others prey on weakness. Even women, who aren't usually told the same things about fear as men, have a hard time discussing fear because they don't want to be judged as insecure.

You see, the problem with this philosophy is that it inhibits us from being able to function at an optimum level. When we ignore fear, we become enslaved to it. We cannot fight an enemy we think is not there. When fear dominates, it creates stress and anxiety, anger and frustration. I have never gotten angry at another person without fear being present. When I am sitting in traffic for an hour, I tend to get a little frustrated. If I try to relax and focus my attention on the true cause of my frustrations, I see that the fear of being late is the driving force. When someone gives me a dirty look and I get a little irritated, I realize fear is involved. When I am frustrated over not having enough money to pay the bills or my kids don't listen to me, I feel fear. It engulfs everything we do, and we have to be aware of it or we cannot face it. Fear is at the root of every negative thought or emotion.

When I first got into recovery, I did not believe I had any fears. I told myself I was not afraid of anything. I was asked by a mentor to make a list of my fears. I thought that was ridiculous. But I made the list with an open mind and decided to write my fears on paper. I realized then that I was afraid of everything, and fear touched every aspect of my life. I was afraid of dying, living, starving, being homeless, being injured, being alone, being talked about, being taken advantage of, being mistreated, being sober, being drunk, being successful, and failing. I was afraid of everything.

But my biggest fear was of being judged. I always worried about what others thought about me, and I always lived on a stage to convince them that I was a good person: good-looking, strong, tough, and honest. I wanted to be accepted and loved. I dressed a certain way to fit in. I talked a certain way to show off. I operated on fear all day long, every second of the day. It dominated me and controlled me. Every word, every thought, and every action started with fear. I could not take responsibility for myself and would rather blame others because I was too afraid to fail. I was afraid to admit I was wrong or that I had problems because others would prey upon my weakness. I became angry, judgmental, and jealous, and I had no self-worth. I would tell myself I was the best thing since sliced bread, but I didn't believe it. When drunk or high, I felt confident, and I could lie to myself. When high, I would believe everything was all right. When sober, I was afraid to deal with life and felt guilt and shame. The more I hurt others, the worse I felt. I couldn't even convince myself that I was a good person anymore at the end. I was afraid to face life and would rather drink and drug then deal with the mess I had created. In this way, fear was destroying me and keeping me sick.

I had a client tell me he was sick of discussing feelings in group therapy sessions because his father taught him that dealing with such issues was for women. I asked him if he liked to work on cars. He said yes. I asked him if he would replace an engine if it was not running properly and if he would give the car a tune-up if it wasn't getting good gas mileage; he said yes again. I asked him if he wanted his life to run smoothly and without error, and he admitted that he would. I asked him why he would not try to remove the things in his life that were effectively giving him poor gas mileage. He understood my point and stated that he could see how removing fear from his life would be beneficial. We remove errors so that we can run effectively and at full capacity. We face our fears because we want peace and safety from using. When we cannot face our fears, we operate on automatic pilot. We act irrationally and hurt others. We become confused and cannot figure out why we are unhappy.

When we are afraid, our system does not operate right, and we become low on courage, faith, and patience. We have no peace when we are standing in fear. It sucks the power out of us and defeats our efforts to help others and to be of service to our Creator.

So, how then do we face and overcome fear? First, we have to get our fears down on paper and then we have to learn to challenge their validity by feeding ourselves with the truth. For example, I challenge my fear of failing by focusing on the truth that I will fail sometimes and succeed other times. But *I* am not a failure. If we are afraid of what others think, we should tell ourselves that some people will think poorly of us and some won't. Remember that our thoughts affect the way we feel, and thinking creates feelings. We need to learn how to think in a more effective way.

Every time I am afraid, I try to look at the reality of the situation. I ask myself if there is a need to be afraid or if my feeling is irrational. To put it another way, do I believe that the lady in a gym is a threat, or am I just feeling insecure and having negative thoughts about the situation? We learn to recognize our negative thoughts and attempt to change them into positive thoughts.

Christians look at God's word and apply it to each situation. God does not believe I am unworthy or a failure. We learn when we read the Bible how God wants us to act and think and to replace our thoughts with Godly thoughts. Jesus provides the strength to challenge our fears and bring them to truth. With his help, we begin to ask God for power and strength and especially guidance, and we believe and have faith that he can change us for the better. We look at facing fears as a chance to grow into the likeness of our Creator. When we learn to deal more effectively with our fears, we experience more peace of mind, and our chances of running to the bottle or our drug are greatly diminished.

Remember, change takes time, and it takes courage and faith to look at our fears. For example, if I am afraid of what others think about me or afraid to be judged, I will have to look at how these fears are affecting me and decide whether they are valid or not. We need to put people in our lives who can help us see the truth about our fears, including friends or professional counselors or therapists.

When I ask my clients about fear, many of them tend to get confused. Many do not even discuss it—it is taboo to do so in a room full of men, for example. It can be very difficult to get a group session going when I bring up the topic of fear. It usually goes like this: I write *fear* on the board, and my clients stare at me for a few minutes, and I have to start the discussion. My clients stare at me because they would never want to admit they are scared, because fear is something we hide at all costs. We believe that admitting fear shows weakness; I believe it shows courage.

Recognizing fear takes practice. We have to start recognizing our innermost feelings. When I am worried about what someone else is thinking about me, I need to recognize it. When I am worried and stressed out about bills, sickness, and failure, I need to recognize it. We act irrationally when our fears overcome us and scream, yell, and lose control. But our greatest trick is to hide from our fears. We develop tools to avoid dealing with it. We protect ourselves by blaming others and convince ourselves that we are okay. I ask my clients to face their fears. We can learn to control them when we see them for what they are. When we recognize fear, it loses its power. If I know I am afraid to be judged, then I can try to challenge and overcome that fear. When I operate on autopilot and let fear run wild, I become enslaved to it. But I cannot act irresponsibly today and blame it on someone else. I have to learn to cope and deal with my emotions in order to be on safer ground. We all get afraid, but we cannot allow fear to dominate and control us.

If you are ready to get to work, then stand tall and face your fears. Christians ask the Lord to give us the courage to face our fears. We pray for his guidance in recognizing them. We know that any life that runs on self-will is powerless and that our fears lock us into a victim position and we cannot exhibit full power in victim mode. We have to take responsibility for changing these habits. We need to understand that fear will rear its ugly head and take back control, but we have a protector. We must have faith that God is in charge. We know he wants us to love our neighbors and does not want us in conflict with those around us. We are to be good examples for others. When we work through our fears, we gain power. Nothing can steal away our peace of mind faster than fear. If you are ready to challenge your fears, say this prayer:

Prayer

Lord, give me the strength to stand against the things that keep me from you. Help me surrender my ability to deal with fear and anxiety. I recognize that fear is Satan's tool. Give me the faith to stand strong. I pray that I will not run from life's worries. I pray that I will not allow my fears to control me. I search for your truth and ask that you show me freedom. Amen.

Here are some samples of my fears and the consequences of not challenging them:

Fear of failure: low self-esteem, depression, and anger

Fear of what others think: low self-esteem, conflict with others, anger, depression, anxiety, and substance use

Fear of not adding up: low self-esteem, depression, anger, anxiety, isolation, lack of motivation, jealousy, and substance use

Fear of being judged: low self-esteem, lack of motivation, anger, feeling like a victim, anxiety, frustration, despair, and substance use

Fear of losing control: anger, frustration, despair, jealousy, controlling behavior, depression, lack of motivation, and substance use.

Fear of change: lack of motivation, lack of discipline, excuse making, focusing on others, and substance use

Fear of being alone: depression, anger, anxiety, and substance use

Fear of intimacy: controlling behavior, lacking trust, abuse, loneliness, depression, and substance use

Fear of letting go of substance use: anger, not being able to take responsibility, blaming others, depression, anxiety, stress, and substance use

Fear of being used: lacking trust, depression, anger, controlling others, and substance use

Fear of being taken advantage of: lacking trust, depression, anger, manipulation, and substance use

Fear of admitting when we are wrong: low self-esteem, blaming others, lacking trust, depression, anger, and substance use

Take some time now to come up with your own list.

CHAPTER 7

Removing Obstacles

Watch and pray, lest you enter into temptation. The spirit indeed is willing but the flesh is weak.

—Matthew 26:41 NKJV

No temptation has overtaken you except such as is common to man; but God is faithful, who will not allow you to be tempted beyond what you are able, but with the temptation will also make the way of escape, that you may be able to bear it.

—1 Corinthians 10:13 NKJV

I asked my clients one day in group therapy to describe the key issues to staying sober. Many stated that recognizing their triggers to using was going to be the most important aspect of their recoveries. A trigger is any thought, place, person, or situation that comes before a desire to use drugs and/or alcohol. I had to learn what areas of life made me most vulnerable to drinking or using drugs. I then had to put my triggers on paper so I could recognize these danger areas and develop a plan to stay sober. Examples of some of my triggers include anger, depression, other negative emotions, bars, emergency rooms where I could get pills, parties, and hanging out with old drinking friends. Whenever I experience one of these things, I tend to think about drinking or using drugs.

Staying sober is very important, and I have learned to avoid these triggers. I need to have the courage to remove anything that blocks me from my goal of living sober and free. Early in my sobriety, I struggled with triggers and did not have a plan to deal with them. I also did not have the courage or desire to make serious changes in my life. I was afraid to exchange what I knew for what I did not understand. I was asked by members of my recovery support group to make changes that I did not have the confidence to make. I continued to relapse because I put myself in bad situations. I did not know how to control my emotions, and I was a slave to depression. I had no coping skills, so I would experience uncomfortable emotions and run to drugs or alcohol.

The biggest area I struggled with in early sobriety was avoiding people who were a detriment to my recovery. I did not have the courage or desire to leave old friends behind and build a new positive support system. I believed I could handle the pressure of hanging out with people who were still using and drinking, so I continued to hang out with them.

When I was twenty-one, the navy sent me to rehab. I struggled with the idea that I could not hang out with old friends. I remember when a friend who also used and his wife visited me in rehab. I knew deep in my heart that I could not hang out with them and stay sober, and I felt hopeless. I wanted to stay sober, but I did not want to make tough decisions. So I started hanging out with them and got high within the week. I had a desire to stay sober, but lacked the courage to make the decision to avoid that particular trigger. It was not their fault that I got high, however; it was my fault for being in a situation that caused a desire to use.

On other occasions, I would purposely hang out with individuals I knew would influence me to drink. Today I don't put myself around people who are not going to accept my decision to stay sober or convince myself that I can hang out with them. I surround myself with godly, positive people who will help me grow and who want the best for me. My sobriety is such a blessing. I do not want to ever put my new found freedom in jeopardy. I don't judge those that drink, but I cannot afford to put myself in a position to fail.

I cannot think of one person in my support system of family and friends today who would try to sabotage my recovery. But to get there, I had to have the courage to make tough decisions. I pray for those old friends who are out there struggling and dying.

I also had to learn to avoid places that would trigger a desire to use. I cannot hang out in bars and other places where drinking or drugging is going on. I don't belong in houses where people are getting intoxicated or at strip clubs where I am setting a bad example for my children. I am around alcohol, however. At Christmas parties, my family is known to have a few drinks, and sometimes I have to go to a wedding where alcohol is present. I pray for God's assistance before the event, and I don't entertain the idea that I can drink like other people. I have to admit that it is uncomfortable at times, but I only put myself in those situations when I can't avoid them. I don't think that everyone in the world has to stop drinking because I have a problem. My family members don't influence me to drink, and I always have the option to leave if I feel uncomfortable.

If I have to go to a place where I am at risk, I always find an escape route in case I get uncomfortable. For example, I might bring a sober friend to a wedding, or I might let my spouse know we are going to leave the minute I get uncomfortable. I ask God to guide me in this area as well. I ask him to give me the courage to stay away or deal with the situation in a positive and effective way. I believe in the Lord, and know he can keep me safe.

The last trigger is thoughts and feelings. As I stated before, irrational fears and negative emotions can be triggers for me to use drugs or drink. If your trigger is being depressed, for example, then you need to deal with this negative feeling so you don't get drunk or high.

We have to understand triggers so we can deal with them effectively. It helped me to get them down on paper so I could get a good look at them. Trying to come up with ways to overcome them took a lot of time and energy, and I found that writing helped me a lot. I was able to write down my feelings and start to develop a plan to cope with them. I then found that positive feelings also created a need to use. Sometimes I would want to drink because it was sunny out, because a child was born, because everyone else seemed to be having fun drinking. Whatever creates a thought and need to use is a trigger. We have to be aware of the negative *and* positive thoughts and emotions that create a desire to use.

I found that a trusted friend, pastor, or therapist was very helpful in this area of change. As a counselor, I teach my clients to challenge and change negative thoughts because we pay attention to how our thoughts create feelings. We have to learn to start sending ourselves positive messages and think more effectively. To do this, I teach clients to build a positive, supportive network. I discuss with them fun things they can do to stay away from negative environments. Finding new friends, new hobbies, and new ways to deal with life is not an easy process, but it is necessary. We must learn to be assertive and let others know we are planning to stay sober. If we want to stay sober, then we have to make tough decisions and not make excuses for our newfound freedom. Many will try to stay sober and fail because they put themselves in situations where using was justified.

When I was a few months sober, I had to make a tough choice. I ran into an old friend, and every instinct told me to get away. I had been preparing for this moment for months. He asked me if I would like to go to a Halloween party with some old friends from high school. I immediately got nervous. I was sober and feeling good. I did not want to go back to my drinking lifestyle, but I said, "Sure, I will see you there." You see, I wanted to stay sober but I did not want to make tough choices. I went to that Halloween party and told him and others that I was not going to drink. I remember my friend saying, "Don't worry, we won't let you drink." But within thirty minutes, one of them put a beer in front of me and I was drinking again.

I don't think they meant any harm. I believe they and others who do things like that don't understand what we are dealing with, or they don't really care.

I have already discussed some of the main culprits for me such as anger, resentment, and fear and discussed how I overcame them by trusting in Jesus. I know today that God's word offers me solutions. I find answers in the Bible that help me deal with triggers. I can ask the Lord for strength and courage to overcome my obstacles.

Most alcoholics and addicts struggle with change. People in general struggle with having the courage to change friends and build a positive social-support system. I honestly can't tell you how many of my clients say, "I am not going to stop hanging out with old friends because we have been friends for years." They discuss how it is going to be impossible for them to stop being around family who are going to expect them to have a few drinks. To make changes or continue on the way we are living is a difficult prospect. But remember there is always fear in change. We are afraid of the unknown. We may be afraid that life will become boring. I see clients struggle with this decision every day. Most of these individuals lack the courage necessary to commit to a life in sobriety because they are afraid to fail.

We have to learn to set boundaries. We need to expect those around us to support our decision to stay sober. If they cannot support our decision, then we have to let them go. I tell clients that sobriety is tough and most people don't have the courage it takes to stay sober. To go on the way we are living or try something new is not an easy decision to make. I was desperate enough. I made the decision to do whatever it took to stay sober. I was willing to let old using friends go, to avoid drinking and using situations, and to take the self-search necessary for recovery. My peace of mind and freedom is the most important thing in my life. I find freedom through my relationship with God. When I stick close to him and grow into his likeness, I have no trouble making tough choices. I know God has a plan for my life and that my sobriety is necessary for it. I have a strong support system today. I found that all the fears I had about change were wrong. I had the courage to try something new and found that life is way more interesting and fun than I ever imagined. I love my life today!

Are you ready to make tough choices? Are you willing to try a new way of life? It takes courage to try something new, and we have to step out in faith. We have to believe we can have a life full of peace and serenity. We must believe that life is going to be worth living in sobriety. Change is hard. We ask Jesus to remove our fear of change.

A life without purpose is no life!

Prayer

Lord, I ask you to remove my fear of change and guide me in the change process. Give me courage to embrace a life with purpose. Give me guidance and strength as I step out into the world of sobriety. Please help me help those who are still struggling. In Jesus' name I pray. Amen.

CHAPTER 8

Freedom from Self and Serving God

Jesus spoke to them saying, "I am the light of the world. He who follows me shall not walk in darkness, but have the light of life."

—John 8:12 NKJV

I came to realize that my selfishness was the main root of most of my problems. I believed the world revolved around me and my corner of it. That little house in Warren, Michigan, was the center of the world, and every time I moved, the center of the world moved with me.

My definition of being selfish is "the inability to see outside of my needs and wants." When I act selfishly, I try to make others fit into my plans and desires. I want the world to do as I say and follow my lead. I try to control others. They in turn rebel and then problems arise. The more the world denies my right to have complete control, the more I fight to get people around me in line. I want them to act the way that I think they should act and behave the way that I believe they should behave. Whenever the world falls out of line with my desires, I get angry, upset, depressed, and irritable. I am always in conflict with people.

Some who read this will get angry and say, "I am not selfish. I am a giving person." My point is that our problems arise out of us; we are always focused on what is going on within us. We need to be responsible and take control of our thoughts and our emotions. We need to make good choices and behave wisely. The problem arises when we cannot see how our actions affect others. We get so focused on how things affect us that we fail to recognize others' rights and we blame them for our problems.

When I am angry, it is usually because people fall out of line with my desires. When I am sad or lonely, I blame others because they did not follow my plans. Whenever I run into conflict, it is because the world does not behave as I think it should. If they would just listen to me then everything would be perfect. Every time I find something unacceptable it is because it goes against my desires, my will. Before I was sober, I never had peace because I was always in conflict. I was never happy because the world seemed like such a horrible place. People were always hurting me, and I was always hurting them. I cannot find peace when I act selfishly. Before I started on the road to sobriety, I could not tolerate others' bad behaviors. I blamed them and told myself that everything was their fault. I had no peace.

Anger, resentments, and frustration dominated my thoughts and controlled the way I felt and acted. I blamed others and gave them complete control over me. I could not stop thinking about the anger and pain they caused me. I had to learn that the world did not revolve around me and my intentions. I had to learn to accept others' rights. I was not that good at making decisions anyway, and my decisions always seemed to get me into trouble. When I act like the master of the world, I pretend to know what is best for other people. My will goes against theirs, and we have problems. I was not put on this earth to become the leader. I could not even control my own life!

I realized a long time ago that any life run on self-will was going to be a complete disaster. I could not control my emotions and was prone to act out. I realize I am in good standing whenever I surrender control of my thoughts, decisions, feelings, and actions to the will of God. I am at peace when I know I am living the way that God wants me to live.

I gain power and peace, strength and courage when I serve God. I know today that my purpose on earth is to live in concert with the will of my Father in heaven. I have surrendered my life over to the care and protection of Jesus Christ. I know today that God has my best interest in hand. I believe he has the power to keep me sober and the desire to teach me how to live a happy and purposeful life.

I used to wonder why people would want to turn their will over to the care of something they could not see or could not understand. Why would I want to surrender control of my life to anyone? Why would God want to have control of my life anyway? I found then that there is power in God, and he gives me that power when I am close to him. When God is in control, we are in a better position to act and react to life's problems. I surrender my control because I believe Jesus will show me truth and give me knowledge and power. I believe God wants me. I believe he designed me to live with him and for him and to serve his purpose and desires. Our Father wants us to come home so that he can throw a grand party. We were designed so that God could have fellowship with us. He calls us to love our neighbors and to serve them. The Bible is a book designed to bring God's word and purpose to our lives. The Bible is the owner's manual.

God Works In All Things

"And we know that all things work together for good to those who love God, to those who are

> called according to his purpose. For whom He
> foreknew, He also predestined to be conformed to
> the image of His Son, that He might be the firstborn
> among many brethren. (Romans 8:28–29 NKJV)

We believe in Romans 8:28, that God will give purpose to our lives. He will make everything that happens in our lives good. My addiction was devastating, and it caused pain to others. But God has been able to make it good for his purpose. He desires us to change more in the image of his son. He wants us to follow Christ's example and live and bring others to the saving knowledge of God. He saves us so that we can save others. He longs to rejoice over our decision to follow him.

It can be hard to surrender one's life over to the care of the Creator. It takes faith. Christians have faith and believe the Lord will provide the tools necessary to live and be free. I have found that surrender takes trust. I trust Jesus. I have learned that progress leads to perfection.

> And he said to all, "If anyone would come after me,
> let him deny himself and take up his cross daily
> and follow me. For whoever would save his life will
> lose it, but whoever loses his life for my sake will
> save it. (Luke 9:23–24 ESV)

When we take up our cross, we are telling the Lord we are willing to struggle and go through trials while trusting him. When we lose our life, we are abandoning it to the care of our Creator, knowing he will provide for us. We know that surrender is power and it takes courage. We believe that Jesus will take our offering seriously and show us peace and mercy. We grow in the likeness of God, and we know peace. Jesus wants us to have faith and trust. He wants us to *accept* him. When we accept Christ's sacrifice and ask him into our lives, we find freedom and power.

The plan of salvation is that Jesus Christ came to earth to die for our sins. He left heaven's luxuries in order to free us from sin. We do not get to heaven as a result of living a good life. Let me say that again. We do not get to heaven as a result of living a good life and being good people. The Bible says that no one is good enough for heaven because we all have sinned and turned away from God. We turn back to our Creator and accept him into our lives. We believe by faith that Jesus came to this earth as God in the flesh and died on a cross. His death released me and all of us from the punishment of sin. The only requirement for membership into the fellowship of believers and a relationship with Jesus is to ask him to forgive you and ask him into your life. I promise you the Lord will not let you down. All that we need is a mustard seed of faith, and he can work with that. I trust Jesus today and know he is protecting me because he loves me. I follow his word to the best of my ability and trust the results to him. He offers forgiveness and strength.

I have found my purpose. I searched for a lifetime to find what was only a few words away.

"Jesus said, 'I am the way, and the truth, and the life. No one comes to the Father except through me'" (John 14:6 ESV).

I am so excited about what God has done in my life that I could write this chapter of the book for a year and not say all I want to say. These final chapters are my main reason for writing the book. Today I live in the solution and not the problem; Jesus is the solution to the problem.

Jesus said no one comes to the Father (God) "except through me." Jesus is the answer. Jesus is the creator of the universe. The Bible says he created the world and eventually the human race. Jesus died for our sins so that we could be free. He produced many miracles to show his power. Even those who did not believe he was God verified his miracles.

If you are ready to accept the Lord into your life, say the sinner's prayer and find freedom. Jesus claims to be the door that leads to the throne of God. He is God. He wants you to believe and have faith in him. He wants fellowship with us. He wants us to serve him and to be like him. He wants to give us his power. He wants us to become his disciples. He is the author of our lives and the ruler or the world. He waits for us to call on him, but he cannot come into our lives without us asking. He is the truth. His word is written in stone. He is the author of history. He will bring his children glory and will give them power to overcome anything. He loves because he is love. He died so that we may live. Will you ask him today to come into your life and bring freedom?

"Behold, I stand at the door, and knock. If any man hears my voice and opens the door, I will come in to him, and will sup with him and he with me" (Revelation 3:20 KJV).

Open the door, for he knocks. He does not want anything but you and to show you how to live a free life. Peace, happiness, power, love, forgiveness, strength, emotional stability, courage, and wisdom are some of the gifts of the Spirit. What are you willing to sacrifice in order to achieve freedom and purpose, love and power? Are you willing to sacrifice the old lifestyle in order to live a blessed life?

Christians know that any life outside the purpose of God is not worth living. We surrender to Jesus because he wants us and loves us. He provides us with the power and peace to stay sober, and we in turn glorify him and do his work. His labor is not hard. Rather, I feel powerful when I am in the will of God.

One day, I felt the Lord asking me to talk to another person about his plan of salvation. I remember being scared, and I didn't want to do it. I was in an argument with this individual about worldly issues, and he was blasting God, saying God is a figment of humanity's imagination and he considered himself an atheist. I asked him a simple question: why are you mad at God?

That question took him by surprise, and he stated, "I am not mad at God!"

I asked him how the world and all of its intricacies made sense without a creator. I asked him if he would allow me to pray for him. He stated that I could. I asked him to pray to God and ask God to reveal himself, and he surprisingly stated that he would. I knew that if he honestly prayed for God to reveal himself, that God would.

I felt power that day. Serving God and helping others is a powerful thing. When I do God's work, I feel his power move through me. I'm not some great author or motivator. I wrote this book to give away what I have been given. I know God is going to work through his children in a mighty way. It is not about being sober. It is about living and growing into the likeness of Jesus Christ.

Getting sober without the power of God is like putting a cartoon Band-Aid on a severed limb. We need the power of God to protect us from evil. We need his grace to get us through the rough spots. We experience power when we are unified with his spirit.

If you are ready for that power, say this prayer and ask Jesus for strength and wisdom. Listen, this is not some pop-culture phenomenon. This is the one who created you. This is not about living a perfect life or an old man in a white robe watching everything you do and judging it. This is about a father's desire to hold his child. God wants you, but he respects you enough to stay away until you ask.

Ask the Lord Jesus into your life. Our relationships with Jesus are personal ones. I have found a loving and forgiving God. Oh by the way, we get the bonus of spending eternity with him in heaven. Look it up.

Sinner's Prayer

Jesus, forgive my sins. You are God in the flesh. I ask you to come into my life and teach me to live a life of purpose. I accept your free gift of salvation. I believe that you died for my sins. I trust that you will give my life meaning, and I ask you to help me to stay sober. I thank you for being patient with me, and I rejoice that you love me. Show me your glory and help me to reach the world. I am not afraid to change. I have your power. Lord Jesus, I cry out to you.

Help me to find purpose, and thank you for your sacrifice on the cross. I cannot wait to spend eternity with you in heaven. I love you. Give me the courage to step out and serve you.

If you said this prayer and meant it in your heart, you are now a child of God. You are saved. The Father welcomes you home. The angels rejoice.

Remember, our lives are not going to be perfect. There are going to be hard times. We may stumble, but we will never fall. We will fall short of God's desires, but he is always there to help put the pieces back together. Living God's way is so much easier and meaningful.

Prayer

Lord, allow me access to your throne. Give me power and the faith to surrender my will to your likeness. Give me the courage to trust you and faith to know that when I open the door, you will supply my needs. I know I will fall short at times. I thank you for your patience. I praise you in every storm. In Jesus' name I pray. Amen.

Conclusion

My story is a one of redemption; I found freedom from addiction by trusting Jesus. I wanted to have fun and live an exciting life full of meaning. I found that drugs and alcohol were only an illusion that provided a temporary relief for life's struggles. I used drugs and alcohol to deal with negative emotions. I lived a selfish life. I bought the lies. My selfish life created misery, pain, anger, depression, resentment, and emptiness. I learned in sobriety to forgive and accept. I learned to trust my higher power. I experience peace and feel love in the arms of my Creator. I gain acceptance and guidance by surrounding myself with positive people. In the end, I found that Jesus was the answer. I embraced God's word and studied the Bible. There, I found freedom. I have a forgiving God.

"For God so loved the world that he gave his only begotten Son; that whoever believes in Him should not perish but have everlasting life" (John 3:16 NKJV).

"Jesus said to him, 'I am the way, the truth and the life. No one comes to the Father except through me'" (John 14:6 NKJV).

Jesus gave his life for us. He chose a brutal death so that we could have freedom. That's love. That is not an old guy looking down from high, ready to strike us down because we make mistakes. Jesus wants us. He wants his children to come back to him. He died for it. Jesus said, "I am the way, the truth and the life." No one gets to the father except through him. No other false gods fit the bill.

I am working to rid myself of the things that block me off from God. I have learned that anger, fear, and resentment keep me out of God's will. I am not close to him when I allow those things in my life. I value myself today because God loves me. I ask God to use me, and I draw closer to him. I avoid the things that can cause me to slip and strive for peace. Life is not easy at times. I fail constantly. I have a desire to grow into the likeness of my creator. I pray for constant guidance. I ask for forgiveness when I fall short, and I am encouraged by my successes. I know I am growing each day. I am a work in progress. I am the clay, and I allow my God to be the potter. My God is patient and loving, and I am safe in his loving arms. We don't need to feel bad about ourselves anymore. God has forgiven us and has a mighty plan for those who come to him. Smile: he is there to help.

I ask you now where you stand. Are you ready to tap into the power that transformed my life?

"The thief does not come except to steal, and to kill, and to destroy. I have come that they may have life, and that they may have it more abundantly" (John 10:10 NKJV)

"So if the Son sets you free, you will be free indeed" (John 8:36 NIV).

We open our hearts to the Lord. We cry out to Jesus. He promises to reveal himself to those who call out his name. We have faith that any life led outside a relationship with God is never a success.

Are you ready to be born again? Are you ready to find salvation in the Lord? No one comes to the Father except by him. He is ready and willing to throw a feast in your honor. The peace that comes with knowing the Lord is at your fingertips and is wonderful. Don't be afraid. The Lord is there to protect you, and he loves you. He wants nothing more than to embrace you. It is so simple. He is a loving father who forgives and gives life. If you are ready, say the Sinner's Prayer.

Jesus, I have sinned against you. I believe that you are God and that you are my salvation. I accept the promise of your salvation. I believe that you died for my sins to bring me life. I ask you to come into my life and show me your will. A life without out you is not worth living. I believe in you. I believe that you died so that I can be forgiven. I surrender myself into your arms. I trust in you. Free me, O Lord, from my chains and bring me freedom. Jesus, I believe that you are my God, and I open up my life to you. Hear me, O Lord. In Jesus' name I pray. Amen.

By saying that prayer, you have ensured your eternity in heaven. You have the peace and power of our Lord Jesus Christ. Things will be hard and you may slip. But remember the Lord is your refuge and shelter. Open your life to that power and be freed.

But it goes further than this. Jesus wants us to live for him and serve him. He wants us to follow him and trust in his power. He calls us to go out and help others. We must make it our mission to share what we have learned. Part of our mission in life becomes serving others. He wants us to teach others about him and to give our friends the message of salvation. We see how our story can save others. The Lord wants his children to come to him and have fellowship. He wants us to live for him. He wants the freedom to enter our lives and clean out the dirt. We make the decision that we are going to grow into his likeness. We read the Bible so we can educate ourselves with his statutes. We learn about God's power and love through his Word.

God does not want his children to suffer anymore. Jesus wants us to come home so that he can have a celebration. The Bible says God will leave ninety-nine sheep behind to find one lost sheep. He awaits you. He wants you. All you have to do is ask, and you shall receive the power of God. I have never known peace and purpose until I embraced the will of God. I am free today because he set me free.